You Are a Spirit

Also by Kayhan Ghodsi

Audio Programs

Meditations for Nine Steps to Heaven on Earth:

A Companion to **You Are a Spirit**

The Magician:

Master of Life

You Are a Spirit

Nine Steps to Heaven on Earth

Kayhan Ghodsi

with Stephanie Gunning

Yaas Press

Modesto, California

Published by Yaas Press.
Email: contact@yaaspress.com
Web: www.yaaspress.com

ISBN 978-0-615-34276-4

Grateful acknowledgment is made for permission to reproduce an excerpt from the poem "Love Is a Funeral Pyre" from *The Gift: Poems by Hafiz the Great Sufi Master*, translation by Daniel Ladinsky. New York: Penguin, 1999.

Printed in the United States of America
Rose illustration: Roya Ghodsi

To John Fulton and David Pearce,

who taught me how to close my eyes and

wake up

Heaven is when there is no fear.

In heaven there is certainty, rather than belief.

Heaven is when we are in our own truth.

Heaven is all there is.

Contents

All the false notions of myself
that once caused fear and pain

have turned to ash
as I neared God

what has risen
from the tangled web of thoughts

now shines with jubilation
through the eyes of angels

—Hafez

Introduction

There is an old Persian proverb that says: "Only what comes from a heart can touch a heart." This book comes from the heart. My prayer is that it shall serve as a mirror so you may learn to see yourself as the mighty spirit you are.

This mirror will not reveal you to yourself as who you think you are (a human or a physical body with which you identify), but as a spirit who is as infinite as its source. This mirror will not tell you that you are only a physical body that can be destroyed by adverse elements, illness, or time. This mirror will not teach you that you are a story with a name, a family, a job, a nationality, and a bank account.

If you choose to look in the mirror I am holding up before you and to study what is reflected there, you'll see that above all you are a spirit.

You'll see very clearly that you were created by the Creator in its image and not as a victim of what happens outside of you.

This mirror will show you that the perfection of the universe has created you perfectly. This mirror will reflect your innocence so you can see it and allow it to guide you back to heaven where you belong. This mirror will demonstrate to you that because you are a spirit you do not have to die to go to heaven.

Because you are a spirit, there is no end to you. You exist in eternity and not in time. Life is all there is—and forever will be. Because you are a spirit, you belong to heaven. You can be there the instant you expand your awareness to include this deepest essence of who you are.

You Are a Spirit is written from the perspective of clairvoyance (clear seeing). It involves two principal things: mental pictures and energy.

To work with your life as a spirit, you'll be playing with your imagination and energy.

Everything discussed in this book takes place in the realm of the physical world because you are a spirit in a body. However, I'll invite you to imagine what exists metaphysically beyond the five-sensory world. The human brain is capable of processing a tremendous amount of information every second. The average person is consciously aware of only a small portion of this. In order to access other parts of your experience you simply have to expand your awareness. You don't have to accept being "average."

But how do we expand our awareness? Our spiritual aspect has little or nothing to do with the physical environment. Therefore, we practice closing our eyes to see what else is present if we do not judge and reject it. By social agreement, we forgot we could do this.

But there is a path to follow that helps us to remember the space of spiritual knowing. In this book, my intention is to guide you through nine steps on this path in order that you may develop confidence in your own ability.

Certainty.

It is human to forget and remember, to forget and remember ... again and again. Not to worry. These nine steps can always be used as a mirror to discern the truth of how powerful, creative, radiant, and wonderful you are.

If you are ready to rediscover yourself as the complete you—the entire package of the human and the being, the physical body and the spiritual body, the person and the spirit—then it is time for you to look into the mirror that is this book. It is time for you to wake up to your holiness.

A Note from the Author

Imagine the most beautiful rose you've ever seen. This rose is a rose of respect, a symbol of our separation. Place it between us as you read this book so you won't take on my energy. We are entering a space of spiritual communication rather than a space of competition.

Please do not automatically believe what I say. Also please do not automatically reject what I say. In this book, I'll offer you considerations. Weigh and test each one in your own life. Take as much time as you need. Everyone grows at his or her own pace. Keep it if you like it, or discard it if you do not. I am not here to impose any beliefs on you.

Dear God, I ask for a miracle today.

I ask for your help so I can see myself as you created me.

I ask for a miracle today.

I ask for your help so I can see myself through your eyes.

So be it.

Amen.

Step 1
You Are a Creator

Imagine that you've gone to a movie, perhaps an action-adventure drama or a romantic comedy. As you sit in your seat in a darkened theater, munching on a tub of buttered popcorn or a box of Jujubes, you find yourself getting so immersed in the events depicted on the screen that you forget you're watching a movie. You feel as if you're actually in it.

As you're watching the pictures that you see projected in front of you, you're having a blast. You're laughing and crying, feeling ecstatic and angry in turns, and really enjoying dissecting the different characters' motivations. It's enthralling, so engaging and believable. Then it's over and the lights come on. You go home either satisfied or dissatisfied, with no confusion that you were just presented a story.

Life is like being at the movie theater, except that as you began watching *this* movie you got up and walked into the screen, and promptly forgot who you are. You now identify so closely with your image on the screen, and with those of the characters around you, that you have forgotten how this story was created for your amusement, for the experience of it.

Perhaps today you'll allow yourself to pull back and entertain, just for a split-second, the idea of being a spirit residing in a human body.

After all, what are you supposed to do when you don't like how the "movie" is going? If you're just a character, you're stuck and out of luck. But if you are willing to consider that not only are you a character playing a role on screen, but also the screenwriter and the director of the movie, then there's always the possibility that you could change the course of events. Your life is like one long, interactive movie in which you can instantly rewrite the script and change the elements of the story.

Here's the secret to living as a spirit in a body: If you consider that you are the creator of your life—in other words, the cause, rather than the effect of your experiences—just by considering this idea, your life changes. That's why this is the first step to heaven on earth.

There's a force in the universe whose entire job is to give you what you want. It's like the electricity that powers the movie theater and makes it possible to turn on the projector that beams light on the movie screen. On an energetic level, your physical body is swimming in this force, which is present in every cell and atom. It's an energy that responds to your imagination and feelings. The minute you say hello to your ability to command this force, your whole life changes. Suddenly you become aware that you are in two places at once: on the screen and in a seat in the theater.

Many people spend time bouncing back and forth between these two points of awareness. It requires no effort to shift to the spiritual view. The force that creates physical reality for you will willingly create this experience at the blink of an eye. And there is no "danger" in shifting your perspective, as your body remains intact. The realm of spirit is a reality that's actually more real than the material world. When you open yourself to the world of spirit, your body becomes a channel for the energy of creation.

Where does experience occur? I am sure you would agree it takes place in the body. If you cannot taste, touch, smell, see, or hear something, you are not having an experience. Since you already are a spirit in a body, you don't have to "leave" it to experience spirit.

When does experience occur? It takes place in the present time. Sure, you may have memories of events from the past, but your experience of remembering those memories is in the present. Yes, you may be able to imagine what the future will hold, but that picture in your mind is being experienced in the present.

Since in this book we're discussing your everyday, physical experience of life, we're always talking about what's going on in the present moment—*now*—in your body. And … get this … if you want to have a new experience in your life (joy, surprise, pain, or whatever else) you'll have to stay with your body. Your body is your cosmic clue to present time. The body cannot go to the past or future.

Your life. Your reality. An experience. Where do they come from? They result from you, *in your physical body*, manifesting something through a combination of mental pictures and energy. You are the creator of your life experience, a person/spirit who has the power to change your destiny and conditions.

The question is, why is it so hard to believe you can do this? Without this ability to create, your life is happening to you, rather than *through* you. You are in a defensive position. You live in fear. You live in a jungle, no man's land, where the fittest triumph. If it is happening *to* you—coming *at* you—you are a victim. This seems like a raw deal.

Well, when I go to Joe and say, "You are creating your own life," he may be reluctant to believe it. It probably is easier (in a way) not to believe it. When he gets outside of his body, by projecting himself into the past or the future, he is disconnecting from his special ability to use this force to create his subjective reality. So Joe may have often had the experience of wanting something that didn't come to him.

Here's the beauty part. Being the creator is not something Joe, you, or I can be or not be. It is what's real. Even stuckness is a creation.

You *can* create anything ... and so, if you occasion to create an experience you don't like, there's no need to attack it or defend against it. Just create something else. If you want the experience, keep on having it. Remember that universal force whose sole purpose is to give us the physical experience of what we want? You are entirely submerged in this force, or energy.

There are three parts of us: the body, the spirit, and the ego. The screen that provides the opportunity to have various life experiences is known as the ego, which is the identity that we make up and present to others as who we are.

My screen identity, the role I play in the movie, is anything I define myself as being: Kayhan, a man who manages a restaurant and teaches clairvoyant meditation courses, a U.S. immigrant originally from Iran, the father of two young women, a photographer, and a lover of Mexican music. What is the role of the ego in creating my life? What is its purpose? It is a necessary element in the process of physical manifestation. Without these specific definitions, I'd be giving different instructions to the force that manifests experience. As a result, I'd likely have a much different life.

The mistake the ego makes is to believe that we are as small as any of these definitions. It's like believing we are Colonel Mustard in the library with the candlestick, from the board game *Clue*, when really we are so big that we are one with God.

The ego does this when we live the reality created by the energy of a lie.

From a clairvoyant perspective, we run the energy of other people through our bodies on a daily basis. In our relationships, for example, we are often running our parents' energy, which is a lie for us. This could be the energy of a mother's unhappiness in her marriage, or a father's pissed-off-ness at his dad. In our careers, especially when we're having trouble liking what we do and doing what we like, it's a sign that we are running someone else's energy (perhaps an expectation), which is a lie for us.

At the moment we run someone else's energy through our body it becomes a lie. It's not a lie *for that person*; it's a lie for us!

My truth = my energy. If one day I pick up my sister's sad energy in Iran, it becomes a lie in my space even though she is halfway around the planet.

At that moment, the flow of the special manifesting force around me becomes static. I stop being able to create my own life, because I'm trying *energetically* to live hers.

A principal time that we stop being the creator of our own life is when someone voices a problem and, instead of watching it, we try to heal it by running that energy through our body. When we fail to respect that other people create their so-called problems in order to have experiences, we lose ourselves in their energy. Then our lives are created from a lie.

Let's say you come to me and tell me you have a horrible headache. If I take on the energy of your pain—running it through my body, thinking I can fix it—I will be the out-of-control healer. I will get a headache, too, *and you'll still have yours*. But if I stay in my body in present time and, as a matter of compassion, offer you a ride to the pharmacy to get some medicine, that's a matter of support. Then I'm not in competition with you and your headache, and I won't lose myself.

Life energy is in motion, and it constantly moves in different directions. If you want to move in a new direction in your life—to get anywhere—a fundamental step is to say hello to your body. If you don't, you are denying your ownership of your physical body, at which point the energy of creation stops creating new experiences for you through that body.

It's important to take baby steps as you move through the considerations in this book. You may want to pause for a day or a week between chapters, so you may fully absorb and process the information you've just read. Also so you can decide if it resonates with you.

Clairvoyance is the realm of pictures and energy. If some new piece of furniture were brought into your house, you wouldn't necessarily keep it, would you? Nor should you take anything I say to heart without testing if it matches your truth.

When you play with my suggestions, imagine that what I'm telling you is a picture in a picture frame. Don't make a decision yet if it's bad or good. Hang it above the mantle and look at it. See how it affects your life. Then decide.

Here, and at the end of every step in the book, you'll find a simple meditation practice to assist you in looking at these pictures.

To begin, I invite you now to sit quietly for about five minutes and say hello to your body and your power as a creator.

Sit in a comfortable chair with your spine supported and both of your feet flat on the floor. Your hands can rest easily on your lap. Take a deep breath and close your eyes. As you close your eyes, become aware of the physical environment around you, the location of your body. Then, notice and say hello to different body parts, like your elbows, the back of your knees, and your collarbones. Sometimes we say hello more often to our shoes than to our feet.

Bring your attention to the center of your head, the area behind your eyes and between your ears. From the center of your head, imagine a rose a few feet in front of you. Allow this rose to represent you as the creator of your life. As you look it, say hello to your body again and see how it feels. Give your body a few moments to get used to this consideration.

Keep breathing and bask in the energy of your creative power for a minute. Then, when you're ready, open your eyes and go about your day as usual.

Do this meditation once a day for a few days in a row and notice if anything shifts for you.

Dear God, I ask for a miracle today.

I ask for your help so I can see that your perfection has created me perfectly.

I ask for a miracle today.

I ask for your help so I can see the perfection in every holy instant of my life.

So be it.

Amen.

Step 2
You Are Perfect in the Present

Perfection is a misunderstood concept. The whole notion of perfection versus imperfection implies a discernment that there is some way things absolutely should be. But who is this arbiter whose expectations "must" be met?

The friendly universal force whose sole function is to translate our energy into physical events always provides us with the perfect life experience in the moment. A sad experience is an experience, as is a happy experience. If you look at both with awareness, neither is bad. Bad and good are irrelevant ideas to the force.

If you sit down and look at your life—your job, career, money, and relationships—consider first that they were perfectly created by this clever force, which gives you what you want—even if you're not conscious of wanting it.

As the mighty spirit you are, the perfection you seek is to express your energy creatively. Yesterday—by being a certain way—you created yourself to be who you are *now*. Yes, believe it or not, today you are exactly what you wanted to be *then*. You're the perfect expression of that creative impulse. And yesterday you were the person that you wanted to be *the day before*.

Similarly, now you face the important question: "Who do I want to be tomorrow?" The future "you" will be a perfect expression of your *current* creative energy.

Can you accept that you are perfectly who you need to be to have the experience you are having? If you were a taller and skinnier person you would have a different experience of life. Two million more in the bank, one million less, or a change in any other aspect of your physical life would entirely shift the experience you are having in your body in present time.

"Okay," you may be saying. "But what do I do when I feel a sense of stuckness and lack of movement?" You might be adamant: "My job is perfect *at the moment*. My finances are perfect *at the moment*. But my relationship *currently* is not." Well, this is a clue you're not seeing the whole picture of how it came to be.

My assertion is that no matter what is happening, the *process* is a perfect process. Whether or not you have a good job, good health, and a mutually supportive relationship, the present is always the ideal creation.

"Perfection" is a loaded word. It is easy to mistake it with someone else's expectations that we'll match up to their ideas of how we are supposed to behave, think, or look, or of what our life circumstances should be.

A main reason you might not have believed you are perfect, until now, is that you were complying with expectations that got placed on you by your parents, family, a spouse, friends, and society at large. Those expectations are lies in your life because they are false for you.

It is rare, indeed, for us to believe we are perfect, although many of us have experienced wonderful moments of flow. It's terribly easy to allow energy from outside sources to bump you out of an optimal state of being. Other people's energy and opinions can be seductive. If ever you have trouble embracing the notion of your own perfection, that's a clue to look again.

Let's use my life as an example of perfection masquerading as imperfection. Right now, I am single. If you go with conventional wisdom, you might guess that I feel lonely or disconnected. In truth, there's perfection for me in the lack of relationship, as it gives me space to explore other aspects of life. I am taking time to pursue activities on my own that I denied myself for years: photography, writing a book, reading, teaching, and calligraphy.

It's important to remember that there are many other aspects to life than a career or relationship, or the possession of money and objects. If you focus on one part of your life and disregard the others, you cannot feel whole.

For example, if you believe a relationship is 95 percent of your life, and it ends, there's a tremendous sense of loss and deprivation. Subjectively, you are now missing 95 percent of your self-image. Although it's painful to feel loss, there is perfection in discovering other facets of your genuine, individual self—in discovering that you are whole, not lacking.

It's common to perceive temporary life circumstances as permanent. In my own case, if I thought being unattached meant I would be alone forever, I might get upset. But I know that it is a choice and I can make a new choice.

Fear comes in and affects your nervous system when you think it's not in your power to change your circumstances. But the minute you affirm your perfection and your choices of how to think, act, and live, your energy changes. Stagnant energy begins to flow again.

It is important to validate yourself, your needs, your desires, your choices, and your experiences because you created them. So, if you're feeling imperfect, ask: "What does this experience (situation, condition, idea, feeling, or "imperfection") offer me in the overall picture of my life? Why have I created this?"

After reminding yourself that on some level of being you got what you requested, do another quick inquiry. Ask: "If I got the experience I wanted, why am I unhappy or discontented? Whose expectations are clouding my perception of this area of my life or my being? What are those expectations?"

As you consider your perfection and affirm your right to choose your individual way of being, allow yourself to release other people's expectations. Quite often becoming aware of an expectation is sufficient to release it's grip.

Running your own energy through your body in the present time is the most authentic, harmonious, and fulfilling way to create a life. Running the energy of someone else's expectations is like drinking sour milk. Drop other people's expectations and you will feel safer, calmer, more satisfied, and more joyful, because your life will begin once again to perfectly reflect your energy for you.

Life is not a game of perfection. Life is a game of awareness. The world will reflect the movement of your energy. Choose.

Raise your awareness of the perfection hidden in any "imperfect" circumstance. Once you free yourself from the lies of social expectations, you'll be able to live the truth of your own energy.

Years ago I read a book by a Sufi author (sadly, I have forgotten the name), who asserted that if, when a poet died, people found out that the result of his life's work was only one verse, that single verse would be sufficient and meaningful if the poet had poured his or her authentic truth and energy into it.

There's perfection in one truthful verse.

When I was studying at the San Francisco Art Institute one of the students made a film that was one frame long. There are 24 frames per second. The film started in black, then suddenly you saw one frame of a haystack and a voice on the sound track said, "Hay!" and then it went back to black. The sound was actually longer than the image.

It was a beautiful movie.

There's perfection in one truthful frame.

Hay.

Likewise, there's perfection in you sitting (or standing) there reading this book right now.

Hey, you.

To conclude our look at step 2, I invite you to sit in silence, as you did at the end of the last chapter. Sit in a comfortable chair with your back upright, and with your feet flat on the floor.

Take a deep breath and close your eyes. Bring your attention to your physical environment, and then say hello to different parts of your body.

After you get comfortably settled, bring your attention to the area between your ears and behind your eyes: the center of your head. From there, imagine a rose a few feet in front of you. Allow this rose to represent the perfection of your creation—your perfection. As you consider the energy of your perfection, say hello to your body again and see how it feels now.

Give your physical body a few moments to get used to this energy. Then, when you're ready, open your eyes and go about your day as usual.

Dear God, I ask for a miracle today.

I ask for your help so I can recognize my physical body as the answer to my prayers, as an environment that brings me the experiences that my knowingness longs for.

I ask for your help so I can be aware of who I am, as I go through the manifestation of life.

So be it.

Amen.

Step 3
You Are Not Your Body

In *Fruits of the Earth* (*Les Nourritures Terrestres*, 1897), the French poet and novelist André Gide wrote: "It is not enough to read that the sand of the beaches feels smooth, I want to feel it with my bare feet." I believe he intended to say that knowledge unprecedented by sensation is of no value to the soul.

As spirits, we truly know everything and have access to the energy of the cosmos, yet we cannot feel the wind blowing through our hair or sense the sun's warmth on our faces unless we have bodies. Without our bodies, we cannot hear a dog bark or listen to music, nor can we see a sunset or an apple orchard in blossom. We need to experience these things so they can affect us and shift our energy. Awareness is the basis of all growth and transformation in our lives.

Our bodies are vehicles for our spirits that give us access to two important experiences. The first is physical experience, using our senses. That's fundamentally what life and having a body is all about. The second is being brought into the moment. The beauty of a body is that it locates us in time and space. It defines where we are in the tangible realm of existence.

The mistake we make, or the deception that is perpetrated upon us through means of social agreement, is that we are bodies exclusively, and when they are gone we will cease to exist. The biggest problem that comes from this kind of over-identification with the body is that it causes us to fear damage and death. We believe when the body is gone we'll be annihilated. This terrifies us so much that we shut down and get stuck. It interferes with creation.

If you realized what the body is and what you are, your relationship with your body would shift. Right now you may fail to honor it for bringing you the chance to do, have, and be what you desire. You may get angry with your body and complain about it, or even blame it for the supposed imperfections of your life. You may forget to be grateful to it on a daily basis.

Every minute counts more when you live in the full realization that you are not your body and one day it will be gone. Adopting this perspective—awareness of the impermanence of the body—gives you an opportunity to savor the moments of your life, to really, deeply appreciate your experiences.

Over-identification with the body results in fear. Identification with the spirit brings us joy. When we take a "risk" to experience the full blast of the life force, it feels phenomenal. We are alive when we use the body fully. This does not mean you have to go bungee jumping. Just letting go of fear and being present in your body is sufficient.

As the mighty spirit that you are, you have a constant desire to expand, to know, to sense, to evolve. Pursuit of that which you desire is a demonstration of love. But we must distinguish pursuit from possession of the object of desire. Possession is not love. Hunger for *experience* is the most important aspect of the equation—and this includes the experience of desiring.

Through the experience of life, you literally become a new you and experience more of what is possible; and this process feels good. As Al-Ghazzali, the renowned Sufi theologian of the eleventh century, wrote in his book *The Alchemy of Happiness*, "Thou mayest measure thousands and thousands of measures of wine, but until thou drink it no pleasure is thine."

The person who learns about wine is not the same person who has taken a drink. The former knows. The latter is transformed.

If you are longing to own a Mercedes-Benz automobile, on an energetic level that's fine. Just don't mistake the Mercedes for the real prize you are seeking, which is experience. The car has meaning to you. It represents a specific energy. But energy takes innumerable forms, and the form of a car changes shape in time.

When you see the car in the showroom, it look shiny and new, and perhaps you get excited. You open the door and smell the clean leather seats. Yes! Then you buy it and take it home, and go for long drives on Sunday afternoons. Through the years that follow, you change the oil, rotate the tires, and wax the hood, nonetheless the floor mat eventually wears out, the knobs come loose, the metal undercarriage rusts, and the car battery dies.

Honoring your desires is life. Don't miss the opportunity to pursue and fulfill your desires. But don't mistake your possessions for you. It is tempting and common for people to measure themselves by how much money they have in the bank, how much stuff they have in the house, what kind of car they drive, and what they wear. But those are just experiences. As a spirit you are senior to your possessions.

Your body is not so different from your car, except that you may not recognize it for what it is: an environment that enables you to walk through the energy field in solid, sensing form.

Your physical experiences are personal and through them you will find your own truth. You will grow and find certainty as you allow them to affect you and alter your sense of who you are. Life is the constant expression of desire for certainty. The minute you intellectually know the sand is soft you want to feel it and be certain of what that is like. And as soon as you experience the sensation of sand this certainty changes you into a new version of yourself.

Imagine that I told you how much I love listening to old Billie Holliday recordings. I go on and on about her songs and voice. Even if you own a state of the art sound system, if you haven't yet listened to her music you only know my feelings about it, not your own. Your knowledge of Billie Holliday is superficial.

Then you listen to Billie Holliday on your sound system. Suddenly you have knowingness. Before, you suspected it would be good. But directly hearing the music turns you into somebody else. Maybe you like it and so you want to hear another album. Or maybe you don't like it and you decide to try something else. In either case, you've been transformed. Now you know yourself as someone who likes or dislikes Billie Holliday. The new "you" that you've become has new desires that the old "you" didn't have as a result of that awareness.

You keep turning into the next version of yourself. If listening to Billie Holliday on your sound system was your desire, the new you will be a "you" who has been validated. You will like this version of "you." However, if you fulfill somebody else's desire, you won't get the validation—it'll go to the other person—and you won't like the new version of "you."

When we see ourselves as bodies without recognizing our spirits we disconnect from the body. As communication fails, the body doesn't know what we want to experience. But when we create from the truth of spirit, we are content. Expanding our awareness to include both our spiritual and our physical bodies enables us to experience our wholeness. From wholeness we create experiences that bring us our truth.

My body is the answer to my prayers because it brings me my truth.

Your body is the answer to your prayers because it enables you to discover your truth.

When you realize that you are a spirit you'll see how your prayers have been answered. You'll look at your body as your artwork. You'll admire it. You'll love it. You'll be grateful.

Transformation takes time because we need to allow for the process of direct experience to occur. Changing into another version of you or of me is an evolution. It's not a competition. It's important for us to be vulnerable enough to allow our experiences to change us on a spiritual level without fighting for or against it. We need only be open and present. The body doesn't make the change occur, the spirit does—although experience initiates it.

If you want to change your life, trust the process of transformation. Just like planting a tree, it is counterproductive to dig up the seed every day and wonder why it isn't growing. No. Fertilize it, water it, and then leave it alone. Change happens when you discover your truth.

At first people tend to disagree with me when I say that we're not bodies. But they misunderstand me. If we identify ourselves with our spirits, it doesn't mean we dislike our bodies or that the spirit and body are in competition. Rather it can be a relationship of respect—with the spirit as a higher authority.

Spirit is the experiencer. The body is the instrument of the experience.

Fortunately for you, although you include your body, you are not only your body. I submit to you that you are someone experiencing being you for a while. And that your spirit has no expectation of being you for eternity any more than you have the expectation of wearing the same pair of shoes for the rest of your life. (Or owning that same Mercedes for the rest of your life.)

Once you truly accept that your body is a part of you that you own, you'll gain a lot of power. You can step out of fear because who you really are is impossible to destroy. You are really the eternal essence of the universe.

Would you be willing to consider that you own your physical body instead of being it? Please spend a few minutes right now looking at your body in the light of this proposition.

Sit upright on a comfortable chair or sofa, with your feet flat on the floor. Close your eyes, relax, and breathe naturally. Say hello to some different parts of your body, such as the back of your knees and the tips of your toes.

Then, bring your attention to the center of your head. From there, see how you extend past your physical body. Consider that the area around your physical body is not empty.

Sit with this consideration for a few minutes. Allow your physical body to get used to you in light of this energy. Keep breathing.

When you're ready, open your eyes and go on with your day. Do this meditation for a few days and see how it affects your life.

Dear God, I ask for a miracle today.

I ask for your help so I can clear all the punishment pictures out of my energy field, and become aware of my freedom and power as a spirit.

I ask for your help so I won't be deceived, and so I won't turn my new awareness against myself in the form of guilt or regret.

So be it.

Amen.

Step 4
Your Vision Sees More than Your Eyes

If you are not only your body, then who are you *really*? You're invited to consider this question. As a mighty spirit, you have tremendous abilities: pure vision (intuition) and pure communication (telepathy). But you won't be able to use either of these gifts consciously until you say hello to them. It's your validation that matters.

Just as your eyes enable your physical body to see, the third-eye at the center of your head gives your spiritual body vision. Your third-eye reads energy, so that you perceive energy vibrations as different colors. On the physical level, you express yourself by making sounds with your vocal cords that ears can hear and make sense of. On the spiritual level, you can "hear" non-auditory messages, and hold conversations with spirits and the deceased.

Everybody has these abilities. The only reason you don't know this already is that you agreed not to know it until today. You can choose to know about your abilities right now.

While physical life relates to survival, to emotions, and to will power (or *chi*—the force capable of moving objects), spiritual life relates to communication, to vision, and to knowingness. As a spirit, you love yourself and you are made of love, and you are capable of compassionate communication. You know things. Life as a spirit is an effortless creation.

As a spirit, you have access to more information than you do as a five-sensory person. Not only can you access pure love, you also have access to communication at any level. Your body and your spirit intersect in the heart center, which is a *being* space, rather than a *doing* space. You are also connected to information and wisdom from the universe through an energy center on top of your head.

You have seven energy centers in your body, known as *chakras,* which run from the base of the spine to the top of your head. Each chakra relates to a certain kind of energy. The three lower ones, located in your torso, are related to physical powers. The three higher ones, located in your neck and head, are related to spiritual abilities. To align with spirit, like turning the dial on a sound amplifier, we must turn down the "volume" on the lower chakras and turn up the "volume" on the higher chakras.

Information and energy are essentially the same from the clairvoyant perspective. Spiritual energy is the energy of awareness.

If for at least a few seconds every day we bring our awareness to the other side of who we are, and say hello to our abilities as a spirit (a being made from love, who has an unlimited ability to communicate, and who can see energy), then for those seconds we have access to all the information associated with the unmanifested aspects of the physical realm.

If the next day we could do it for a few seconds more, and the day after that for a few seconds more, suddenly our lives would change. Just by saying hello to ourselves as spirits we become wiser. We can become aware of who we really are throughout an entire day.

We do not have to associate with the part of us that feels as if we're constantly in survival mode, at the mercy of our emotions, and can only do things by means of force. Rather, we can be in the mode of love and introduce the energy of being-at-no-effort to our daily lives.

Everything that becomes manifested results from something that exists in the unmanifested world. We are able to connect with that realm more and more easily once we become aware of our spiritual nature. By reminding ourselves, at intervals, of our connection to the force of creation we begin to notice that we are feeling less fearful and expending less effort to manifest what we want. We learn that we can make things happen with little or no effort.

Heaven is not a strange place that you will go to when you die. It's here right now. Using the energy of spirit you can immediately affect the physical realm of your existence. You can communicate on a spiritual level with others. You can also use your vision and knowingness to transform your life. If you say hello to yourself, you can be in heaven and connected to your physical body at the same time.

The beauty of connecting to your spiritual powers is that you affect the world without force. For example, if you are annoyed with a friend, you don't have to call your friend on the phone and argue your point of view. Instead you can say hello to your friend at the fifth chakra level (the power center located in your throat) and engage in gentle spiritual communication. Your communication won't emanate from survival needs and emotionality, from force. It will emanate just from your spiritual hello. This kind of communication in the intangible realm is a part of our daily life and it always has been.

Spiritual communication has no limits. We can communicate with the universe, with a plant, or with an animal, as much as with a friend.

Darkness also does not affect clairvoyant vision. Once you embrace your power of seeing with your inner sight, you'll be able to see energy, including unmanifested energy, and you'll be able to manipulate it. If you say hello to yourself as a spirit, you'll recognize your ability to "see," know, and accomplish everything.

Once you embrace that you are more than your body, you'll become aware of all kinds of things you're already doing on the spiritual level, such as manifesting what you want. When my computer broke a few months ago, I took it to my local computer shop where the repairperson was challenged to respond to my needs. I decided to align with my spirit and patiently wait to see what would come to pass.

I could easily have been annoyed and let my frustration dictate my actions and my speech, and create the events from my lower chakras. I also could have given up and left the shop. Instead I decided to sit nearby on a chair and tune-in to my higher chakras, basically being in communion with the entire universe and trusting that all would be well. I removed force from the situation by floating a boundary rose between the repairperson and myself. That way, whatever happened would happen without judgment and at no effort.

Within a few minutes, another repairperson came over, did a little fiddling with the machine, and solved the problem easily. It cost me nothing. When I asked, "How much does this cost?" he said, "Don't worry about it."

Several years ago, I borrowed some audiotapes from the library of Marianne Williamson's lectures, which I would listen to while commuting to and from work in my car. On one of these tapes, I heard Williamson tell the story of how she was ill early in her career. The way I remember the story, she prayed and prayed for a healing, but nothing happened. Finally, in frustration, she decided to go to a local bar and order an orange juice.

While she was sitting at the bar nursing her juice she struck up a conversation with the guy next to her. It turned out he was a physician. She told him what was up with her body. He pulled out his prescription pad right then and there, and wrote her a prescription. She left the bar, filled the prescription at the local pharmacy, and within a day or so felt better.

Let's say that God made this healing happen as a result of Williamson's prayer. Because she was not on a spiritual level to accept an instantaneous healing, he gave her the healing at the level she could receive it: via a prescription from a doctor whom she met in a bar. Similarly, my computer didn't have an instantaneous healing, because when I first walked into the computer store I wasn't on a spiritual level to receive it. I had to open myself for the help to occur.

The number one principle of the ego is that "I am separate from everybody else." It tells me that a dollar belongs to me or belongs to you, whereas spirit always says that a dollar belongs to everybody. We are part of the same whole. If we go the route of the ego, the mind tells us that we are limited and then we experience limited results. When we say hello to ourselves as spirits, those perceived limitations disappear. There are no limits to the universe or silence or communication in silence.

More than manifesting a TV, a computer, or a parking space, you could actually start manifesting stuff that really fulfills you simply by dropping into the space of being a spirit. When you align with the body, your mind tells you that you have to do and have in order to *be*. When you are aligned with spirit, you *know* that you have to be in order to *do* or to *have*.

Sit upright on a comfortable chair, with your feet flat on the floor. Close your eyes, relax, and breathe naturally. Say hello to some different parts of your body, such as your elbows, the tops of your thighs, and the soles of your feet.

Bring your attention to the center of your head. From the center of your head, imagine that you are looking at a screen a few feet in front of you. On this screen, imagine a picture of yourself sitting in your seat, just as you are, as if you were looking into a mirror.

Seeing an outline of your body on the screen is good enough for this purpose.

For a few moments, practice looking at your image while you stay in the center of your head.

Allow the image to be on the screen and yourself to be in the center of your head. Say hello to your image. But don't go to the screen. Just look at it. Practice seeing without trying to become part of what you're looking at.

Enjoy watching your image on the screen for a few minutes, and then open your eyes. Do this meditation a few days in a row.

Dear God, I ask for a miracle today.

I ask for your help so I can open my inner eyes and see that since creation my essence has been one with all that is created.

I ask for a miracle today.

I ask for your help so I can see that you are that which connects me to All That Is.

So be it.

Amen.

Step 5
You Are One with All That Is

As Rumi wrote, "There is nothing in the universe that you are not. So look inside for everything you are looking for." You are one with everything in existence.

If you felt resistance rise up in you as you read the preceding words (a picture in your mind with the word "no" attached to it), don't worry. It's a perfectly natural response. That picture (No, *no*, NO!), is a "sacrifice" picture. Meaning, it says you must sacrifice something you have in order to gain something else.

Its purpose? To preserve the status quo.

The biggest confusion we all share is mistaking *being* with having and doing. We don't believe we can be one and have body/self.

That's why when people are told that they are one with everything their first reaction often is to reject the idea. "Not true!" they assert. "I have fingers and toes. I have a unique history as an individual." They reply with a long list of items to prove their separateness.

God forbid we should mistake one person's smallness for the smallness of someone else!

They might protest, "I am *not* one with war, hatred, and prejudice." Or: "I am *not* one with *those people*, who believe *those ideas* … look *like that* … eat *that* … practice *that religion*."

With every rejection they become smaller.

Perhaps you actually celebrated when you read the words "There is nothing in the universe that you are not." You exclaimed, "Right on!" and threw your hands up in the air.

Okay. You're on a good path. And … I still recommend that you check inside for even the tiniest hint of disbelief. Hints of disbelief stand between you and full acceptance of yourself as a spirit in oneness. Saying hello to doubting energy will enable you to let it go effortlessly.

What I'm saying is not intended to diminish affirmative responses. I'm merely pointing out that fear pictures get lit up in our minds when this concept is discussed. On some level we all think that agreement with oneness means the possibility of having to sacrifice our identity.

The universe is a big place. Our bodies are tiny in comparison. Nonetheless, our individual internal reality seems *enormous* to each of us. In fact, it is everything we know! That's why we believe that we have something to lose by broadening our self-definition to include more.

We're confused. We've got it backwards.

Really by broadening our perspective we have *everything* to gain. This perspective creates room for you and for me to grow.

I am not my possessions and the things I use to define myself. And neither are you. I am not my car, my clothes, or my job. You are not your house or your children. We are not our religions or nationalities. We are much more.

Whereas in truth we are immense and powerful, each of our stories is little. When we commit to a little story, we put ourselves into competition with reality. Such competition is the root source of stuckness in our lives, and of disharmony and conflict between people.

In this step, we're looking at being one with all that is—the moon and the stars, the air and the trees—and we're asking what it signifies. What does it mean to have ownership of the universe? Ownership comes with the ability to call forth anything that exists and make it part of our life experience. It means we can bring new elements into our lives whenever we want, as long as we recognize that we know how.

Physical reality is like having a dream. My dream is that I am Kayhan, a man with a specific family and career, although at essence I am everything. If I dissect my being down to the smallest fundamental particle, what am I? What's the pure essence of me or of you? It's not this dream—or even recognizably human. On a physical level, it is quantum energy, which is the essence of everything in the universe.

To me, this indicates I have unlimited freedom and mind-bending potential. It signifies that you and I are collaborators, part of a spiritual team, rather than competitors.

If you don't realize that you are one with everybody and everything, then you are facing a bit of a dilemma. You may begin seeing yourself as "better than" or "worse than" anything to which you compare yourself.

Here's the trouble with that. If you are five-foot-two, you're shorter than five-foot-six. How do you *feel* about it? What do you *think*? Once a comparison is made, judgment begins. You decide, "It is worse to be five-foot-six than to be six feet tall" or vice versa, "It is better to be..." Separation is the start of competition.

If I judge you as "tall" and decide that tallness is *not* a good quality, I am in competition with reality. I am requesting you to be different than you are and implying I could do a better job of being you than you are doing yourself. Essentially I am saying, "If I was in charge of your life you'd be shorter."

If I don't accept your height as it is (or any other quality), I am not really saying hello to who you are. We're not really communicating. And there is a likelihood that we'll have conflict.

Once I decide not to get into competition with other things, and not to judge people, then I can extend myself to everyone and everything. If I am not judging you "unworthy of my love," then communication can start between us.

Remember, you are everything. Yes, you are sad, but you are also happy. Yes, you are tall, but you are also short. If you decide you have to sacrifice sadness (or to compete with the reality of sadness) in order to have happiness, then you will go into resistance of sadness.

Now, if you are also aware at the moment of feeling sadness that happiness is there for you, your resistance will simply disintegrate. There is no sacrifice. No competition. No conflict.

Your image of yourself is grounded in your beliefs. Your thoughts constantly affirm that you are who you believe you are. They move in the direction of proving you right. So you could invest in being right about being one ... or BIG.

Moving from separation to oneness is an act of self-healing. It is a shift in perspective that enables us to relate to the world and our life experience with greater mastery. As we move towards oneness, we expand the limits of our vision. We give ourselves permission to view our distinctions on a bigger movie screen, and thus we actually *refine our individuality*. We become more of who we are, rather than less.

When we are in resistance to being one, the things we fight to be right about are often ridiculous. For example, we tend to defend our smallness, rather than promoting our greatness. We brag about it and act as if it makes us special. And if someone tells us we are bigger or have the potential to become bigger and less limited, we feel invalidated by his or her vision of who we are and get mad.

The experience that opened my eyes to this phenomenon in my own life took place at the end of my clairvoyant training program. I looked at John, my teacher, as a higher being, and I "knew"

I would never be as good as him. One day his secretary called me and asked if I would come teach a class with him. I got scared and said, "I don't think I am ready for that."

The next time I saw John he seemed disappointed. I told him I was sorry. He replied, "You've been sitting in that chair in my classroom teaching all year long, and now you won't stand in front of the class and teach alongside me."

Even though I believed John was a more accomplished clairvoyant than me, I was in competition with his idea of my capabilities. In trying to maintain my form and occupy the same amount of space in my life, I refused to take the step of growing into the potential that John was mirroring for me.

Fake humility, that's what it was. It reminds me of a story from ancient Persia written by the poet Saadi. In the story, a young man wanted to become the disciple of a famous Sufi master. He went to the mosque and declared his intention. The master instructed him to take a broom and clean the mosque. Without a word, the man got up and left.

A few days later the master saw the young man in the road. He scolded him, "You are so arrogant. You came to me to become a disciple. Yet, when I asked you to clean, you disobeyed me."

The young man answered him, "Master. You told me to clean the mosque, and I did obey you. For the most unclean thing in the mosque was I."

It's a funny story, which can be perceived from different perspectives. In the East, the young man's answer is viewed as demonstrating his great humility. Easterners are taught that being humble means to see yourself as unclean and base. In the

West, we are taught that being humble means relinquishment and submission.

My current definition of humility is: allowing yourself to change, rather than pushing yourself to change.

Was the guy really smarter than his master? After John's invitation, I pondered Saadi's story. I asked, "Can I humble myself enough to stand beside him?" He was inviting me to stand there and to grow. All I really had to do was to show up and see what happened. I didn't have to know ahead of time how it would be.

The Sufi master could see that the young man was worthy of being a disciple. He didn't view him as unclean. He could see positive qualities in the man, but he wanted him to start his discipleship from a certain place. By saying, "I know better than you do—I am unclean," the disciple was in competition with his master's view of him.

John and I discussed my refusal to take the next step as a clairvoyant meditation teacher. It took about a year before I was ready, but then, with his mentoring of me, I did begin to teach.

Becoming aware of your real (BIG) identity, as you may be starting to see, is about changing your relationship to reality. It is not about getting and having more stuff. However, beneficial experiences—such as joy, peace, and manifestation—will flow from the presumption that your real identity is being one with all.

Manifestation of anything is about focusing on who you are. Take the example of money. If you think about being as wealthy as you are, you will *be* wealthy. It's not that wealth didn't exist in you before. You have always been poverty and wealth, sadness and joy, wind, water, and soil, because you are everything.

Concentrating on one distinction brings that aspect of who you are forward. You are everything and everything is one thing, but you have chosen—like the rest of us—only a few things to be out of all available options. You have chosen to be who you are right now: a person who has a specific job, a specific career, specific relationships, and specific abilities.

Your choices brought those qualities forth in your experience. If you are identifying closely with those distinctions, at some moment in the past it's clear you forgot you had other aspects.

In addition to limiting your options, the trouble with making change when you're in competition with reality is that it requires tremendous effort. A big step in spiritual growth is the step of the relinquishment of force. Effortlessness comes from surrendering to your connection and oneness with all that is.

Ego (the part of us that identifies with the story of our smallness and separateness) tells us that everything in life happens only if we push it to happen. But that's not really how things happen. Everything happens on its own as part of the totality of what happens.

No effort is required to be what we are. As we align with different distinctions, those aspects (mirrored in the world around us) come more into the foreground of our lives. We experience love in the world when we focus on the love we are. We experience cooperation when we focus on our cooperation. We experience peace outside when we are at peace inside. We manifest from near and far.

We learn to trust this effortlessness the more we pay attention to its occurrence.

As we take the step of moving from separation to oneness, we learn that we have two basic choices of how to respond to the world. We can continue employing the world as a projection of our imagination or we can use it as a mirror. The first way is to look at the world and all its contents as a separate entity, which influences and affects us. The second way—from the perspective of oneness—is to look at the world as an extension of our being, which reveals whatever is going on inside of us.

When we understand that we are one, and begin to use the world as a mirror, we see qualities we have not forgiven in ourselves in others, and this is a reminder to us to accept and forgive ourselves.

That is how we grow. Not by refusal. Not by overcoming. Not through effort. Rather by embracing, allowing, forgiving, and humbly accepting what the mirror reveals to us.

I invite you to sit quietly now for a few minutes. Begin, as always, by sitting comfortably, closing your eyes, breathing naturally, and saying hello to your body.

Become aware of where you are, and then bring your attention to the center of your head. From the center of your head, start listening to your heartbeat. Allow it to demonstrate to you how the rhythm of life comes through you, and the life force itself manifests through you.

Also allow yourself to become aware that the life force moving through you is the same force that manifests through everything else. This energy makes you one with All That Is.

Sit with this awareness for a minute or two. When you're ready, open your eyes and go about your day as usual.

Do this meditation for a few days in a row.

Dear God, I ask for a miracle today.

I ask for your help so I can become aware that there is nothing separating me from my brother and sister.

So be it.

Amen.

Step 6
You Have No Problems

As the manager of a restaurant, I have a physically demanding job. I'm constantly walking around, from table to kitchen to bathroom to host-stand to bar to liquor cage to freezer. My job places heavy demands on my body. So I have developed a tendency of sitting down and saying, "I am too old for this!"

Altogether we have a hundred employees and there's always forty people working. Some days I believe that if I heard my name ("Kayhan…" "Kayhan…" "Kayhan…") one more time, I'd drop dead on the spot. It would be so easy to say I hate the job. But when I put aside expectations and look at what the job gives me, it is tremendous. It gives me what I need to have, including being able to help the employees. People constantly talk to me and seek my guidance. From their point of view, there is a perfect reason I am there. My presence answers their need. And where else could I have met them?

The restaurant provides me with a place to practice what I love to practice. I have a passion about food. Even though our kitchen is not the same as the kitchen was in my old restaurant, Café Select, in Berkeley, if a customer complains, I respond, "I'll cook it for you myself." When I cook alongside the cooks, I realize how much I still enjoy being in the kitchen. These are aspects of my energy.

Without the act of judgment, we would have no problems. Knowing we are spirits and have everything, there is no problem. It is only when we take on a judgment, and begin running that energy through the body, that our energy becomes static. It stops flowing the moment we own a judgment. Then we have a problem!

When we judge, "I need to be better than this! My hair is too long! I need to be thinner than this!" not only are we in competition with reality, we are in competition with ourselves.

Judgment affects our ability to have what we want in our lives. When we forget we are pure, unlimited love, neutral and, on a deep, abiding level, at one with everything in creation, then we go into competition with ourselves.

The way you create the next object of your desire is by looking at a "mock up" of it on your mental screen. It is a thought-picture before it is a solid object. The amount of time it takes to appear depends on how much you are ready to have the experience on the physical level. And your ability to create that experience also depends on your ability to see the thing you want clearly.

Here's an example. Let's say you have a boyfriend who doesn't please you very much.

From the clairvoyant perspective, you haven't yet created the boyfriend who would please you tremendously. This means that when you are looking at the image of your ideal boyfriend on your mental screen, there is something blocking your view, an obstruction. Some energy other than your own is defining how that picture looks.

Energy is information. When we run it through our bodies, it often becomes ours. Then we defend it and begin to make it real. If it is energy that contains a judgment or a lie of any kind, it blocks our vision. We then lose the ability to read energy and choose what would make us the happiest.

The purpose of this step on the path to heaven is to see this process occurring and be amused by it. Every time you look at a supposed "problem" ask, "Where is the lie?"

By declaring anything a problem, we distance ourselves from it. This buys us time to heal the part of us that won't enable us to receive that thing. For instance, if you think you are having problems in your career, you can be sure there is a lie blocking you from having the perfect career. Once you see it clearly, you can choose to release it.

Every time you come across a problem smile. Make this your practice. If you were looking at life through a camera lens, you could say you were looking at every problem through a filter. When you smile at the problem, it is as if you have taken off the filter.

If you engage with energy and frown at it with negative judgment, you are screwed. Instead, the minute judgment pops into your mind—*zing*—smile. Please be amused.

Sit in a comfortable chair, with your spine erect and your feet flat on the floor. Take a deep breath and close your eyes.

First, bring your attention to the center of your head. From there, choose a problem. Then, imagine a rose a few feet in front of you and allow it to represent that problem.

As you are sitting in the center of your head and looking at your problem, make a decision. Decide to give up your resistance to the rose, and just to let it be what it is. If anything tells you not to do this, simply be amused.

The purpose of this meditation is to help you give up your resistance to the energy of the rose for a moment or two. Then, when you are ready, open your eyes and go about your day.

Do the same meditation for a few days in a row and see if your problem changes. You may choose a different problem each day or stay with the same one.

Dear God, I ask for a miracle today.

I ask for your help so I can release my resistance to what life brings me and see the gift in every event of my life.

So be it.

Amen.

Step 7
You Can Choose Joy

My daughter Roya got sick when she was three. We were picnicking in a park in Berkeley when my wife and I discovered that she wouldn't eat. She was getting sick—and it only got worse. After a week, she developed a high fever. I came home one day and my wife told me that Roya had been sleeping for twenty hours straight.

We took her to Oakland Children's Hospital, where the doctors did a bunch of tests on her that must have been very scary from the point of view of a toddler. They took a urine sample with a catheter, then strapped her down on a table and took an X-ray of her chest.

Even though it was a horrible ordeal, my wife and I felt happy when the doctors told us they thought Roya had pneumonia. Now we knew what it was and how it could be treated! The doctors gave Roya an injection, put her on a course of antibiotics, and sent us home.

Unfortunately, there was no change in Roya's condition. If anything, she got worse. She hadn't eaten voluntarily in a month, so she was very weak. Most of the time she was passed out. Once a lively, happy baby, now she was silent and mostly inactive.

We took Roya back to the hospital, where she was given a spinal tap and diagnosed with either meningitis or viral encephalitis. Upon admitting her to the intensive care unit, the hospital placed Roya in a special room for contagious diseases. Everyone had to wear masks and we had to wash our hands a lot.

My wife was breastfeeding our other, younger daughter, so she had to be home much of the time. I stayed with Roya every night, and my wife came during the day. Mornings I would rush home and take a shower.

Roya lay unconscious for twelve days. She had tubes running through her to feed her and keep her hydrated. She didn't talk. She didn't move. Seven different doctors took five million blood tests. At this point, they just didn't know what to do. Roya was simply dying and I felt so helpless. My heart ached with grief. Roya was so fragile, so vulnerable.

I can remember sitting there and thinking, "She's dying and I don't know why."

It was two o'clock in the morning. I decided to go outside to get a breath of fresh air in the quiet darkness of the night.

And I don't know why it happened, but in an instant my vibration suddenly changed. For no reason, I went from sadness to joy. And the thing that the joy gave me in such a deeply sad moment was an opening to talk to God.

Something lifted. In sadness, I'd been sitting around wondering why my child was dying and why it was happening to me. After my energy changed, I was in an opposite space. I accepted my situation. There was something else I could do besides sitting around smoking and waiting for death to take Roya. I could talk to God.

"I don't know what's happening," I said, "but if somebody has to die, let it be me."

I finished my break and went back inside. Roya was awake. Normally she cried and had a headache when she woke up. She would be given a baby Tylenol through a tube and pass out again. But this time she woke up and wasn't crying. She was gazing up at me.

I told Roya, "I'm going to talk to you and if you can understand me blink your eyes." She blinked her eyes. We started communicating.

"I know you are scared of all these things around you," I continued, "but you don't need to be afraid. These people are trying to help you. You haven't eaten for weeks. If I get you some scrambled eggs (her favorite food), will you eat them?" She blinked her eyes. I ran to the cafeteria, but it was closed then, at four in the morning.

I got into the car and drove over to Jack in the Box. Roya was asleep when I got back with the eggs. She woke up and I gave her a little bit, about a half spoonful. "Okay, do you want to go home?" I asked. "If I take you home will you get better?" She blinked. I called the doctor and told him I wanted to take her home. It took twelve hours for the doctor in charge to agree. Even so, I knew things were going to change for the better because communication was occurring.

Downstairs, I buckled Roya into the car seat. On the way she didn't utter a sound. But, when we turned the corner of our street, in her tiny, immature baby voice she said, "We're home." After that, things slowly improved. She had to learn how to walk again; otherwise she was a healthy three-year-old.

Looking back at it from a clairvoyant perspective, that night outside the hospital I dropped my resistance to my life and gave up trying to control it. As a result, my vibration naturally altered: I chose joy.

Joy is not caused by external occurrences. It's a state of being, rather than an emotion. It's not the same thing as feeling pleasure or being happy, though some people find joy to be pleasurable. It is an internally produced state, a neutral state that lies beyond the ego. It's always there and available to us, and, in fact, is calling us to discover more about being spirits.

A Course in Miracles says, "God placed in the mind the call to joy. This call is so strong that the ego always dissolves at its sound." *In my case, once the ego lost its hold on me the reality around me shifted.*

I've given thought to how reality bends and reorganizes itself when our vibration shifts to the frequency of joy. That night outside the hospital, I feel certain that I went away. I mean, assuming I am a spirit who has fallen into the screen at the movie theater, the storyline ceased to exist. Joy made me not need to experience the theater.

That's a clairvoyant reading of the situation.

Throughout this book, we've been looking at different types of energy and we've been considering the point-of-view that we are the creators of our reality. If we aim to control life through different chakras, or energy centers, we are trying to control our lives through the lens of survival, emotions, sexuality, or force. Some people try to control through love, others through communication. But really our true center of creation is the crown chakra, which is where we connect with divine energy.

Changing a situation in life does not come from changing what you do, but from changing your vibration. You just have to reset the color of your crown chakra. If you say, for example, "I hate my job. I wish I were doing a different job," but you switch employers and do not switch your vibration, you'll hate the next job as much as the first one. Your crown chakra makes your environment feel good to you.

If you do not choose to set your own color, energy, and vibration, another energy in your space will become senior to yours—you will be influenced to match it. This energy, which could be the energy of your mother, father, or life partner, will determine your vibration and, thus, the kind of environment you live in.

Choosing joy means selecting your own vibration and emotional reality. This really is not hard to do. The first step is just being aware of the space you are in. Accept it—be neutral—and you'll be empowered to initiate change.

Resistance is the main obstacle you're going to face to shifting your energy. If you decide life shouldn't be like it is and focus on what you don't like about it, you will begin taking on the vibration of whatever you're focusing on.

Here's my personal discovery. The beauty of saying hello to God, my Source, is that something can step in to help me when I do. All I have to do is say hello to that force, and it does the rest. And I'm confident that if you see what's coming at you and change your vibration to joy, answers will be there for you just as they are for me.

To reiterate, when I'm speaking about joy I am not describing happiness. I am drawing a word from my homemade dictionary. From this perspective, you could have the emotion of sadness and be joyful too. Joy is like a flame inside us that has the capacity to melt icebergs.

Joy is the unimpeded flow of the life force.

We're always having a conversation with the invisible spiritual world around us. When we're in the frequency of joy, we do not lose ourselves in those conversations. We do not give up our seniority to the energy that continually comes at us. We remain conscious of who we are and our own, genuine energy creates the form of the environment we see.

When we trust in our strength, we are living from the ego, which would have us believe that we have to push to make the world take shape. Whereas when we trust in the life force, changing the world is effortless.

Imagine it like this. You own a house with two rooms. One room is blue. The other room is red. When you tell me, "My sister made me mad, and..." going on and on about your story of being unhappy, it is as if you're in the red room. Joy is like being in the blue room. Now I am telling you that becoming joyful is as simple as walking from one room into the next.

You can stay mad and still walk into the blue room. It's not about your story or what happened or what you do; it is about the color you are. Joy is a state of being. You also don't have to try to give up your story. Just trust that when you walk in the other room, the situation will naturally change.

I invite you to sit quietly for a few minutes. Begin this meditation, as always, by sitting comfortably erect with both feet planted on the floor. Close your eyes, breathe naturally, and bring your attention to the center of your head. Say hello to different parts of your body.

From the center of your head, bring your awareness to the very top of your head. This is the location of an energy center known as the crown chakra, which connects you to the spiritual energy of the cosmos. While staying in the center of your head, imagine your crown chakra turning blue. See how that feels.

Then, make the top of your head brown. See how that feels. Is it any different?

Say hello to your ability to change the color of your crown chakra at will. Sit with this consideration for a minute, and then, whenever you feel ready, open your eyes.

Do this meditation for a few days in a row. As you practice changing the color of your crown chakra, see how a wide variety of colors feel to you. Try any colors you like. Observe whether or not those colors feel familiar to you.

Dear God, I ask for a miracle today.

I ask for your help so I can see that my power lies in my awareness of your constant presence.

So be it.

Amen.

Step 8
You Can Experience Forgiveness

Clairvoyance is a process of looking at energy. Throughout the nine steps to heaven, we've been looking at our energy and learning how to clear it of other people's energy for one important reason: Other people's energy mixed in with ours obstructs our view, and doesn't let us see and accept our innocence.

As spirits, we are entirely innocent. Because we are part of God there is nothing to forgive and never could be. Even the worst villain on Earth is part of God. You may have done things you regret. You (or someone you know) may have made mistakes in the past. Still, you (or that someone) are a divine spirit.

Most of us have a picture of guilt that hovers in front of us continuously like the menu bar on a computer screen. This picture is a part of everything we see and do. It doesn't matter who affirms our spiritual perfection; until we forgive ourselves, this picture makes itself a part of everything in our lives. It colors our choices, activities, and relationships.

Forgiveness helps us see our innocence and forever afterwards changes our view of … everything.

When we are born, we forget who we are and we soon come to believe that we are a character in a life story. As we take on the energy of the people around us, from time to time—because the ego thinks we should be able to control the world and the flow of life around us—we feel guilty for what has happened. Guilt is a decision we make a nanosecond before we run another person's energy through our body.

A child hit by a car feels guilt and runs the remorseful energy of the driver who hit him.

A teenage girl whose parents are in a bitter divorce feels guilt and then runs her mom's anger at her dad.

A man in the street feels guilt and runs the energy of a beggar he passes on his way to work.

Their choices are colored by the energy they run.

Once we make a split-second decision to own a problem, to make ourselves responsible, we begin to think the energy we are running is our own energy. So we must remember, other people's energy in our space is a lie for us—whether that energy belongs to a loving person we admire or to an "enemy."

As spirits we are here to have our own experiences. Direct experiences teach us how we can become the next versions of ourselves, versions that know what we do and don't like, what we do and don't want, and how we intend to live. If we feel guilty (aka are taking ownership of a situation or experience that does not belong to us) we are living in an untruthful way.

Living a lie can never feel as fulfilling as living in harmony with the truth of our spirit, demonstrating the truth of our being with every breath and action.

Forgiveness is to release energy that is not ours. We can do this by going back to the decision that preceded taking the energy on and holding it up to the light of awareness. When we do not reject the truth of something that has happened, it is possible to find our space and discover our own point of view.

Resistance to the truth causes us pain. We resist the reality of ugliness, destruction, violence, poverty, and loss. Forgiveness requires us to stop distancing ourselves, to move closer and be present with reality. The ego believes this will hurt us—even destroy us—and yet the opposite is actually true. It liberates us!

Here's an example. In June 2009, people in Iran took to the streets to protest the results of the elections. Police came out in full force with tear gas, clubs, and guns to stop them from demonstrating. One of the people shot down was a young woman. A video of her lying in the streets bleeding was widely circulated by the news media, where I saw it.

The young woman's death so distressed me that I could not sleep for several days. I was equating the woman's death with my own private sense of loss, imagining how it would be in the future if one of my daughters were killed. I kept resisting the event and was in pain from competing with the reality of what had happened.

Finally, I spoke with a trusted friend who advised me to go to the event psychically and find my space within it. By taking myself to the street where the woman lay dying—during a meditation—and saying hello to her spirit leaving her body and my feelings about what happened there, my pain dissolved. I found peace.

Where was my guilt in this experience? As a healer, I was attempting to take responsibility for the conditions in Iran by running the energy of the demonstrators through my body. But this energy was not mine to own. I have my own truth in relationship to events in Iran, my own energy, and I did not need to run the energy of the young woman's father. I also did not need to run the energy of the people who were so angry with the police for shooting her.

Forgiveness is the closest thing on Earth to the truth of love. Love is a state of being and an energy that transcends the duality of right and wrong. Love is to see the essence of the spirit behind the movie screen where your life is being projected. Love is to see the essence of the spirit in everyone else.

No matter how angry you are, no matter how victimized you may feel, you can realize your wholeness by remembering that you are a spirit. As a spirit no harm can come to you in the body. So you see, there is nothing to forgive. Everyone is innocent.

Does forgiveness mean that we condone violence and the acts of those who perpetrate violence? No. But those acts can help point us in the direction of remembering our true nature. They can bring us one step closer to recognition of our divine oneness.

It is never the person we despise, it is always the act that is despicable. We may hate that a certain capability exists within us, and we may fear its expression. But it is the energy that runs through a person and not actually the person that is the killer or the betrayer. We do not like mistakes, but mistakes are forgivable. Even very big ones can be accepted.

Not celebrated! Accepted. You don't have to befriend people who have behaved in a heinous way. But resistance to their actions is a sign that you have taken on guilt for not having stopped them or predicted what was coming or healed them or reached them… and this means you are running false energy.

You do not have to force this understanding of your innocence on yourself. Let it percolate and rise to the surface of your consciousness in its own time. Let everything that stands between you and your spiritual essence drop away. You are a loving, divine spirit.

There is no way we can bring forgiveness to anyone or to any situation if we don't believe in our own innocence. If we cannot forgive ourselves, we cannot forgive others. Whenever a mistake occurs, that picture of guilt pops up and makes it impossible.

Sit quietly with your feet flat on the floor and your spine erect. Take a deep breath, and then go ahead and close your eyes. Bring your attention to the center of your head and, from there, become aware of where you are and aware of your body. Say hello to it.

From the center of your head, watch your breath for a few moments—the inhalation and exhalation—doing nothing to change it.

Then, also from the center of your head, imagine the top of your head turning gold. See how it feels when your crown chakra is golden.

If you happen to see the color change again without your instruction to do so, simply be amused and bring back the golden color.

Be gentle and allow your body to get used to the golden vibration slowly. Make a decision to let go of your resistance to this energy. Bask in it for a few minutes before opening your eyes.

Do this meditation for a few days in a row and see if it has any affect on your daily life.

Dear God, I ask for a miracle today.

I ask for your help so I can understand that I can put my trust in you during every moment of my life.

Dear God, please walk with me.

So be it.

Amen.

Step 9
You Are in Heaven ... Because You Never Left It

Our last step is to trust God as we would trust the dearest of our dear friends. It is only with total trust that we stop refusing God's love and accept who we are: divine creators of our lives.

We are safe and we are loved just as we are. Our needs are continuously and effortlessly being met within the conditions of our lives. By letting go of competition with the flow of life moving around and through us, we allow God to remind us that we have never left our spiritual home; we have only been pretending to be separate from each other and God.

As we relinquish our efforts to control life, the pretense ends; there are no more fears, only certainty. Where nothing but certainty and absolute faith exists, this is heaven.

The state of being that we call heaven is a state we can enter at any time of day or night. Most of us go in and out of it, forgetting and then remembering with astonishment and gratitude. Going to heaven is not something that happens when you die. It happens both during and after life. It is not that you are body now and sprit later—you're always a spirit.

Heaven is everywhere and every-now.

Like forgiveness, heaven is for everyone. It's not a reward for everyone else except you. Heaven is your natural state of being. You belong to heaven. Heaven—and God—is in you. Your little mind doesn't have to run the whole show, the show runs itself ... and you're part of the show of the evolving universe in motion.

If you see a pop-up picture from your early religious training in your mental space that tells you otherwise, then take a deep a breath. And keep on breathing. I'm just suggesting considerations. Often we're in competition with our better selves and we resist knowing who we are. The picture of heaven for many people is as a reward that exists someplace else, not here.

Heaven is a space that we can live from, like the driver's seat of a car. Like choosing joy, as we bring any of our so-called problems into this space, suddenly we see ourselves as capable of dealing with them in another way.

One of the things about heaven that we need to reflect upon to understand it is that it is a poetic space. Each time I have observed it, I have seen a feeling or a color or stillness and silence. It is metaphorical, symbolic, like a poem. Heaven is beyond words. Trying to delineate heaven shifts us to another space.

Here are some of the qualities of heaven.

The sound is silence.

The color is every color.

The feeling is soft.

Need doesn't exist in heaven—you can have everything you want just by imagining it.

Heaven is a state of overcoming death with a simple change of mind. There's no anxiety in heaven because there's no future. There's no regret because there is no past. It's main characteristic is the gentleness that comes from the absence of fear. It's safe because there is an absence of danger.

It's like being home.

Welcome home.

You have reached a point where you're going to have a different relationship with God. All you have to do to come into the space we call heaven is to "choose once again," as *A Course in Miracles* instructs. In every holy instant, you can and must choose anew. You can choose to be God's friend and to trust.

Heaven is the space where there are no lies. The biggest lie of all that we have to let go of to be in heaven is that God is there to judge us. God is not a judge. That's the lie. God is here to love us. We have trouble loving ourselves because we misperceive God as a judge and we worry that we're doing something wrong out of pain or ignorance. It's a defensive posture. We judge ourselves so God won't have to.

God is our best friend, who loves us unconditionally. The only one who can teach us unconditional love is God, and the space in which we can learn to love is heaven. Until we reach this space, we can't really see who God is. Until we do, we can't really see ourselves.

Throughout this book, we've been examining corners of heaven, facets of heaven. Let's drop all misconceptions and drop all lies about God at step 9. Once we get rid of the lies we learned, we are able to see that God has always been giving us love. We betrayed this love by taking on lies, but God doesn't care.

When we reject our own love, this is blasphemy. Through the flow of life, God says to us, "Love yourself, because I love you."

Think about it carefully now. If God is perfect, all knowing, all seeing, and all-powerful, and God created the world perfectly, then you are perfect. Everyone is perfect.

It is not for us to contradict God and compete with God's omniscient view of us. To believe in your limitations and the smallness of your view of yourself is a form of arrogance. It means you believe you know better than God who you are.

In heaven, we can see ourselves. We can see we're worthy. We can see our holiness. And that's the state of being where we move beyond words and concepts and into nothing but love.

God invites us to go one step further than belief, and enter the ultimate space where there is nothing but knowingness and certainty.

And yes . . . during a really bad day of scrounging for money or wearing shoes that hurt your feet you can still go into that space. Moments will occur in that space when, just because you look at your holiness and vibrate at that vibration, your life changes. Your job, your relationships, your havingness, and the color of your crown chakra will change.

Heaven is not a space of doing, however. It is the pure space of being. Just by sitting in that vibration and looking at your holiness and being there you'll have instances in which everything changes effortlessly around you.

Everything starts here and ends here in the healing space of beingness we call heaven. Being is a process that has no beginning and end. Our awareness dips into it like a pool of cool, healing water and it refreshes our spirit.

I invite you to sit quietly for a few minutes and hold the following considerations in mind.

Begin, as usual, by comfortably seating yourself on a chair or a couch that supports your spine to be upright, and place your feet flat on the floor. Take a deep breath and close your eyes. Bring your attention to the center of your head, then say hello to your physical environment. Become aware of where you are.

Next, say hello to different parts of your physical body. Feel and experience your presence inside your body. And, from inside your body, become aware of your breath.

Then, send a hello to the God of your heart. By this I mean God as you define God, not as someone else would define God. Also open yourself to receive a hello back.

Allow the vibration of God's hello to you to resonate in your physical and spiritual body. Let go and let this energy run itself. Consider trusting the energy. And, if it feels right, say a silent prayer:

"Dear God, please walk with me."

Immerse yourself in the energy you sense for a few minutes before opening your eyes. Realize that you can be in this space all the time if you wish. When you're ready, take a deep breath, wiggle your fingers and toes, open your eyes, and come out of the meditation.

A Final Consideration

If the one I am looking for is the same one that's doing the looking, how do I find the one who is doing the looking? How do I find me?

I choose to let go of everything that tells me that I am not me. All this I forgive. And I shall shine a light in the dark corners where I hated myself. I choose to release all hateful thoughts.

I do not believe I need them any longer.

I am an idea in God's mind. All is an idea in God's mind. I am one with all.

So be it.

Amen.

Acknowledgments

I would like to take this opportunity to thank every ancient and modern poet, author, and teacher who ever helped me move closer to knowing who I am, where I come from, and why I am here, as this book is a result of that knowingness. From Rumi to Voltaire, from *The Conference of the Birds* to *A Course In Miracles*, from Hafez to André Gide, and from Saadi to Deepak Chopra, from Marianne Williamson to John Fulton and David Pearce.

Above all others, I must thank three beings, one of whom is in physical manifestation in present time, and two who are with us only in their spiritual bodies. Stephanie Gunning, my coauthor, who so graciously accepted my humble invitation to take this journey with me and describe the scenery. What a tireless companion she was; her description of the scenery is simply fabulous.

Then there are Elahe Ghodsi, my late sister, and Mohammad Massumkhani, my best friend forever. These two passed when I was in my early twenties, but through tenacity of purpose we were able to grow together. They have helped me tremendously over the years whenever I needed help and grounding.

So, thank you, Elly, thank you, Mammad, and thank you, Stephanie.

I would also like to thank the students in the different meditation programs I've taught (who are too numerous to mention individually, but who are not forgotten) for helping me to develop and refine my thoughts on being a spirit in a human body, and the many readers who looked at early drafts of the manuscript and offered generous feedback. With your assistance this has become a much better book than it would have been otherwise.

May it be with the blessing of the Supreme Being that *You Are a Spirit* will benefit all of us in our spiritual growth awareness and understanding.

Amen.

About Kayhan Ghodsi

Kayhan Ghodsi is a clairvoyant healer and meditation teacher who lives in California's Central Valley region. Born in Iran, he earned degrees in filmmaking from L'Ecole Superieure D'Etudes Cinematographique in Paris and the San Francisco Art Institute. Subsequently, he worked as a freelance camera operator and documentary television and film producer. In 1988, he opened Café Select in Berkeley, California. He studied meditation and healing at the Berkeley Psychic Institute and the Church of Aesclepion Healing in San Rafael, California. In 1999, he began teaching. Kayhan may be contacted at www.youareaspirit.com.

About Stephanie Gunning

Stephanie Gunning is a writer, nonfiction editor, and publishing consultant specializing in books on spirituality, new thought, and healing. Her A-list clients include bestselling authors, major publishing firms, top caliber literary agencies, and innovative small presses.

A certified Reiki master-teacher, Stephanie is co-creator of the popular 30-day online course Stop Thinking Now and host of The Great American Think Out, an annual nationwide meditation event. A graduate of Amherst College, Stephanie lives in New York City. To find out more about her books, audio programs, and services, visit: www.stephaniegunning.com.

Are You Ready to Wake up?

Now that you understand you are a spirit, you're ready to experience the information in this book on a deeper level. To help you see the energy of your own truth through the practice of daily meditation, I created two audio programs.

Meditations for Nine Steps to Heaven on Earth

As a human being, there is a dimension to you other than your physical body. In this audio companion to *You Are a Spirit*, I guide you through nine short daily meditations, considerations that help you get to know your spiritual aspect. You belong to heaven and can be there at all times if you bring yourself to look at the reflection of your Creator's holiness in you. These nine steps can help you change your mind about who you really are, and help you to understand that the kingdom of heaven is you.

The Magician: Master of Life

Your thoughts constantly bring forth life experiences that accommodate your social agreements. When you find the space within you where the thinking mind is listening, not thinking, you have the power to create life based on your divine inspirations. In these four meditations, I help you to look at the process of how you can make new life choices.

Visit www.youareaspirit.com for more information.

These titles are also available on amazon.com

www.ingramcontent.com/pod-product-compliance
Lightning Source LLC
LaVergne TN
LVHW090958080826
845145LV00003B/1044